I0422112

Copyright © Andreas Sofroniou, 2020.

Aristocracy Plutocrats Philanthropy

ISBN: **978-0-244-87989-1**

Contents   *Page*

Aristocracy Plutocrats Philanthropy

Aristocracy

The 'the rule of the best' was originally a form of government, but now usually a hereditary social elite.

From Plato and Aristotle onwards, it was commonly assumed that political power was best placed in the hands of those who, through education, occupation, or social position, had shown their capacity to exercise it.

This assumption was challenged by the democratic sentiments nurtured by the American and French Revolutions (1776 and 1789); the latter provoking, in books such as Edmund Burke's *Reflections on the Revolution in France* (1790) and Louis de Bonald's *Theory of Power* (1796), some of the last explicit defences of aristocracy. The term now describes a hereditary social class, normally based on landed property.

Aristocracy therefore is a form of government that places strength in the hands of a small, privileged ruling class. In practice, aristocracy often leads to hereditary government, after which the hereditary monarch appoints officers as they see fit.

However, the term was first used by ancient Greeks such as Aristotle and Plato, who used it to describe a system where only the best of the citizens, chosen through a careful process of selection, would become rulers, and hereditary rule would actually have been forbidden, unless the rulers' children performed best and were better endowed with the attributes that make a person fit to rule compared with every other citizen in the polity.

Hereditary rule is more related to Oligarchy, a corrupted form of Aristocracy where there is rule by a few, but not by the best.

Plato, Socrates, Aristotle, Xenophon and Spartans considered Aristocracy (the ideal form of rule by the few) to be inherently better than the ideal form of rule by the many (Democracy), but they also considered the corrupted form of Aristocracy (Oligarchy) to be worse than the corrupted form of Democracy.

This belief was rooted in the assumption that the masses could only produce average policy, while the best of men could produce the best policy, if they were indeed the best of men.

At the time of the word's origins in ancient Greece, the Greeks conceived it as rule by the best qualified citizens—and often contrasted it favourably with monarchy, rule by an individual.

In later times, aristocracy was usually seen as rule by a privileged group, the aristocratic class, and has since been contrasted with democracy. The idea of hybrid forms which have aspects of both aristocracy and democracy are in use in the parliamentary form of government and in republics.

There are no pure democracies in the world today, nor have there been since the fall of Athens. There are some governments that have elements of democracy, but all of these are mixed governments, such as the countries of the United Kingdom, Switzerland, Germany, France and the U.S.A.

All this have elements of Democracy, Aristocracy and Monarchy, with a system of checks and balances, where each element monitors the excesses of the other. Therefore, varying degrees of aristocracy are prevalent throughout nearly all modern governments.

Aristocracy can be considered a social class that a particular society considers its highest order. In many states, the aristocracy included the upper class of people (*aristocrats*) with hereditary rank and titles. In European societies, aristocracy has often coincided with the nobility, a specific class that arose in the Middle Ages, but the term "aristocracy" is sometimes also applied to other elite societies.

An aristocratic government places political power in a comparatively small part of the population of the state. This class may be based on birth, wealth, age, military power, priestly power, education, or a combination of these and similar distinctions.

However the ruling class may be selected in an aristocracy the mass of the people are exuded from any effective share in government. Many writers, from Plato and Aristotle down, believed that aristocracy was the best form of government, provided that the ruling class is composed of those most competent to govern and that they exercised their power for the good of all and not for their own selfish interests.

Some who have opposed class distinctions based on birth and wealth have believed in a natural aristocracy of ability and character which should exercise a dominant influence in politics and have believed that government should be so organised as to give opportunity for this natural aristocracy to rise to political power.

The line between aristocracy and democracy is difficult to draw, but the theory of aristocracy has no confidence in the political ability of the masses and believes in government by the select few, relatively small privileged class or by a minority consisting of those felt to be best qualified to rule.

Such a form of government differs from the rule of one (by a monarchy or by a tyrant), of the ambitious self-interested, or greedy few or of the many. For these reasons, the term *aristocracy* often is used to mean the ruling upper layer of a stratified group.

Thus, the upper ranks of the government form the political aristocracy of the state; the stratum of the highest religious dignitaries constitutes the aristocracy of the church; and the richest captains of industry and finance constitute an aristocracy of economic wealth.

The distinction between aristocracy of birth and non-hereditary aristocracy is relative, because even in caste societies some low-born persons climb into the higher castes and some high-born persons slide into the lower castes. On the other hand, even in open aristocracies there is a tendency for the upper stratum to become a hereditary group filled mainly by the offspring of aristocratic parents.

For example, among millionaires and billionaires living in the United States at the beginning of the 21st century, the percentage born of wealthy parents is notably higher than among American millionaires of the mid-19th century.

Oligarchy

Oligarchy is a form of power structure in which power rests with a small number of people. These people may be distinguished by nobility, wealth, education or corporate, religious, p olitical, or military control. Such states are often controlled by families who pass their influence from one generation to the next, but inheritance is not a necessary condition of oligarchy.

Throughout history, oligarchies have often been tyrannical, relying on public obedience or oppression to exist. Aristotle pioneered the use of the term as meaning rule by the rich, for which another term commonly used today, is plutocracy.

In the early 20th century democracies have a tendency to turn into oligarchies; a necessary division of labour leading to the establishment of a ruling class mostly concerned with protecting their own power.

Autocratic leadership

Autocratic leadership, also known as authoritarian leadership, is a leadership style characterized by individual control over all decisions and little input from group members. Autocratic leaders typically make choices based on their ideas and judgments and rarely accept advice from followers. Autocratic leadership involves absolute, authoritarian control over a group.

Like other leadership styles, the autocratic style has both some benefits and some weaknesses. While those who rely on this approach heavily are often seen as bossy or dictator-like; this level of control can have benefits and be useful in certain situations. When and where the authoritarian style is most useful can depend on factors such as the situation, the type of task the group is working on, and characteristics of the team members.

Characteristics of Autocratic Leadership

Some of the primary characteristics of autocratic leadership include:

- Little or no input from group members,
- Leaders make almost all of the decisions,

- Group leaders dictate all the work methods and processes,
- Group members are rarely trusted with decisions or important tasks,
- Work tends to be highly structured and very rigid,
- Creativity and out-of-the box thinking tend to be discouraged,
- Rules are important and tend to be clearly outlined and communicated.

Benefits

- Can make decisions quickly, especially in stress-filled situations,
- Clear chain of command, oversight,
- Good where strong, directive leadership is needed.

Drawbacks

- Discourages group input,
- Can impair morale and lead to resentment,
- May impair or ignore creative solutions and expertise from subordinates.

Benefits of Autocratic Leadership

The autocratic style tends to sound quite negative. It certainly can be when overused or applied to the wrong groups or situations. However, autocratic leadership can be beneficial in some instances, such as when decisions need to be made quickly without consulting with a large group of people. Some projects require strong leadership to get things accomplished quickly and efficiently.

When the leader is the most knowledgeable person in the group, the autocratic style can lead to fast and effective decisions.

Downsides of Autocratic Leadership

While autocratic leadership can be beneficial at times, there are also many instances where this leadership style can be problematic.

People who abuse an autocratic leadership style are often viewed as bossy, controlling, and dictatorial. This can sometimes result in resentment among group members.

Group members can end up feeling that they have no input or say in how things or done, and this can be particularly problematic when skilled and capable members of a team are left feeling that their knowledge and contributions are undermined.

Common problems with autocratic leadership

This style tends to discourage group input. Because autocratic leaders make decisions without consulting the group, people in the group may dislike that they are unable to contribute ideas. Researchers have also found that autocratic leadership often results in a lack of creative solutions to problems, which can ultimately hurt the group from performing.

Autocratic leaders tend to overlook the knowledge and expertise that group members might bring to the situation. Failing to consult with other team members in such situations hurts the overall success of the group.

Autocratic leadership can also impair the morale of the group in some cases. People tend to feel happier and perform better when they feel like they are making contributions to the future of the group. Since autocratic leaders typically do not allow input from team members, followers start to feel dissatisfied and stifled.

Benefits of autocratic style

Autocratic style can be beneficial in some settings, but also has its pitfalls and is not appropriate for every setting and with every group.

If this tends to be the dominant leadership style, there are things that should be considered:

- Listen to team members,

- Establish clear rules,

- Provide the group with the knowledge and tools they need,

- Be reliable,

- Recognize success.

While autocratic leadership does have some potential pitfalls, leaders can learn to use elements of this style wisely.

For example, an autocratic style can be used effectively in situations where the leader is the most knowledgeable member of the group or has access to information that other members of the group do not.

Instead of wasting valuable time consulting with less knowledgeable team members, the expert leader can quickly make decisions that are in the best interest of the group.

Autocratic leadership is often most effective when balancing this style with other approaches including democratic or transformational styles can often lead to better group performance.

Anarchism

Anarchism is a radical political movement that is highly sceptical towards authority and rejects all involuntary, coercive forms of hierarchy. It calls for the abolition of the state which it holds to be undesirable, unnecessary and harmful. Anarchism advocates for the replacement of the state with stateless societies or other forms of free associations.

The timeline of anarchism stretches back to prehistory when people lived in anarchistic societies long before the establishment of formal states, kingdoms or empires. With the rise of organised hierarchical bodies, scepticism towards authority also rose, but it was not until the 19th century a self-conscious political movement was formed.

During the latest half of 19th and the first decades of 20th century, the anarchist movement flourished to most parts of the world and had a significant role in worker's struggles for emancipation.

Various branches of anarchism were espoused during those times. Anarchists took part in several revolutions, most notably in the Spanish Civil War, where they were crushed by the fascist forces in 1939, marking the end of the classical era of anarchism. In the last decades of the 20th century and into the 21st century, the anarchist movement has been resurgent once more.

Anarchism employs various tactics in order to meet its ideal ends; these can be broadly separated in revolutionary and evolutionary tactics. There is significant overlap between the two legs which are merely descriptive. Revolutionary tactics aim to bring down authority and state, and have taken a violent turn in the past. Evolutionary tactics aim to prefigure what an anarchist society would be like.

Anarchist thought, criticism and praxis has played a part in diverse fields of human society. Criticism of anarchism mainly focuses on it being internally inconsistent, violent and utopian.

Groups and classes

Elite

Elite is a select group or social class.

The Italian theorists Pareto and Gaetano Mosca (1858-1941) maintained in a series of influential writings that social groups and societies were inevitably headed by elites: the classless societies advocated by Marxists were impossible.

The German sociologist Robert Michels (1876-1936) argued that even political parties with democratic aims would come to be dominated by elites through the 'iron law of oligarchy'.

The existence of elites in the USA has been much discussed, as they are sometimes held to undermine its democratic basis. Charles Wright Mills in *The Power Elite* (1956) pointed to the domination of the USA by elite from business, political, and military life which he termed the military-industrial complex.

Elites may be forced to change their character. In newly independent countries the revolutionary elites which have fought for change may, after a struggle, be displaced by the next more pragmatic generation.

Elites which do not renew themselves by recruiting new members and remaining open to talent risk, as Mosca held, 'exhaustion that is wont to bring on great social cataclysms'.

Arguably the rigid exclusivity of the governing elites of the communist regimes in Eastern Europe and the former Soviet Union contributed to their downfall in 1989 and 1991.

Social class

Social class is a division or order of society.

Many observers have distinguished between the systems of social stratification found in pre-industrial societies, in which distinctions are primarily of rank and rest on long-established rights and duties, and the systems found in industrialized societies which are based on social class.

In *The Communist Manifesto* (1848) Marx identified classes in relation to the means of production. In capitalist societies, the dominant class, 'the bourgeoisie', owned the means of production, while 'the proletariat' laboured, their surplus production belonging not to themselves but to the bourgeoisie.

For Marx, the criterion of class was economic. Weber, who, with Marx, has strongly influenced 20th-century debate, defined the term more broadly to refer to an individual's ability to command resources: class position might be determined by skills as well as property. Weber also regarded status as a factor in social stratification.

Mid-20th-century sociologists took up the idea of status to the point where some, especially in the USA, denied the existence of clear economic class divisions in their country, while in communist states, classless societies were predicted.

However, evidence from across the world suggests that social class divisions based on occupation and economic standing are to be found in every society. Class position is linked not only to command of private goods such as cars or household appliances, but also to access to resources such as health care, education, and housing.

Democracy

Democracy is a system of government in which sovereignty rests with the whole people, who rule either directly or through representatives.

In the contemporary world, democracy is closely associated with the idea of choosing governments by periodic free multiparty elections, but in the past it was understood more literally to mean the people gathering together in an assembly to debate political issues and enact laws.

As such, it was compared unfavourably to monarchy and aristocracy by most political thinkers, who saw it as unruly and inexpert, and also as impractical in societies bigger than the city-state.

The representative system appeared to solve these problems (although it was fiercely criticized by Rousseau, the greatest theorist of democracy).

The chief elements of representative democracy are:

- freedom of speech and expression;

- periodic free elections to the legislature, in which all citizens are entitled to vote and to stand for office;

- the right to form competing parties to contest these elections;

- a government which is responsible to the legislature, and thereby to some degree responsive to public opinion.

Where one or more of these elements is absent, as in the 'People's Democracies', the one-party states of the communist bloc in the period following World War II, the system is unlikely to be genuinely democratic.

Within the representative democracies, the major issue has been whether increased popular participation, through referenda and other such devices, might make these states more democratic in the original sense.

There has also been pressure for more democracy at a lower level, particularly in the way that work is organised.

The social conditions for stable democratic government have been extensively discussed, with level of economic development apparently the most important single factor: the advanced capitalist societies are nearly all representative democracies, whereas many developing societies (India being a striking exception) have authoritarian governments, despite often laying claim to a democratic structure.

Monarchy

Monarchy as a rule is commonly hereditary, by or in the name of a single individual whereas, absolute monarchs wielding unlimited authority were once the norm throughout Europe, but are now rare.

Most contemporary monarchs are constitutional rulers, with severely limited or even purely ceremonial powers.

Succession to the position of monarch is usually hereditary though other methods, including election, have been known.

The association of monarchy with aristocracy and privilege can be politically divisive, but constitutional monarchs are often effective symbols of national unity above party politics.

Nobles and Gentlemen

European Countries

Between persistent poverty and the prevailing aristocratic spirit several connections can be made. The strong appeal of noble status and values was a force working generally against the pursuit of wealth and the investment that was to lead, precociously and exceptionally in Britain, to the Industrial Revolution.

In France a nobleman could lose rank (*dérogeance*) by working, which inhibited him from engaging in any but a few specified enterprises. The typical relationship between landed gentleman and peasant producer was still feudal; whether represented by a range of rights and dues or by the more rigorous form of serfdom, it encouraged acceptance of the status quo in agriculture.

Every state in Europe, except some Swiss cantons, recognized some form of nobility whose privileges were protected by law. Possession of land was a characteristic mark and aspiration of the elites.

The use of the two terms nobleman and gentleman indicates the difficulty of definition. The terms were loosely used to mark the essential distinction between members of an upper class and the rest.

In France, above knights and esquires without distinctive title, ranged barons, viscounts, counts and marquises; until the summit was reached with dukes and princes of the blood.

In Britain, by contrast, only peers of the realm, whether entitled duke, marquess, earl, or baron, had corporate status: numbering under 200, they enjoyed few special privileges beyond membership of the House of Lords.

The gentry, however, with assured social position, knighthoods, armorial bearings, and estates, were the equivalent of Continental nobles.

With the nobility, they owned more than three-quarters of the land: in contrast, in France by 1789 the nobility owned barely a third. In northern and Eastern Europe, where the social structure was generally simpler than in the west, nobles—*dvoriane* in Russia, *szlachta* in Poland and Hungary—were numerous. In these countries, many of those technically noble were in reality of little importance and might even, like the "barefoot *szlachta*," have no land.

Such differences apart, there were rights and privileges that most Continental nobles possessed and values to which most subscribed. The right to wear a sword, to bear a crested coat of arms, to retain a special pew in church, to enjoy such precedence on formal occasions as rank prescribed, and to have if necessary a privileged form of trial would all seem to the noble inherent and natural.

As landowner he enjoyed rights over peasants, not least as judge in his own court. In France, parts of

Germany, Italy, and Spain, even if he did not own the land, he could as lord still benefit from feudal dues. He could hope for special favours from his sovereign or other patron in the form of a pension or office. There were vital exemptions, as from billeting soldiers and—most valuable—from taxation.

The effectiveness of governments can be measured by the extent to which they breached this principle: in France, for example, in the 18th century by the *dixième* and *vingtième* taxes, effectively on income; belatedly, in Poland, where nobles paid no tax until the chimney tax of 1775.

Generally they could expect favourable treatment: special schools, privileges at university, preferment in the church, commissions in the army. They could assume that a sovereign, while encroaching on their rights, would yet share their values.

Through social pre-eminence, nobles maintained—and in the 18th century even tightened—their hold on the commanding heights in church and state.

Major philosophical contributors

Pareto, Vilfredo (1848-1923)

An Italian economist and sociologist, Pareto's work as a sociologist emphasised the role of elites; more important is his pioneering contribution to economics, where he achieved a fusion of welfare economics with the general equilibrium analysis pioneered by Walras.

In *Course of Political Economy* (1906), he was concerned to demonstrate in what precise sense a system of ideally functioning markets generates maximum social welfare, on the assumption that utility, or satisfaction, is not a measurable and inter-personally comparable substance, but merely a shorthand way of referring to individuals' subjective preference scales ('ordinal' as opposed to 'cardinal' utility).

In other words, any individual is assumed able to choose between any two alternative consumption bundles, and in so doing maximizes utility. Pareto showed that in certain specified conditions the market system generates a situation, now called a Pareto optimum, in which no single consumer can be made subjectively better off without making at least one other worse off.

Plato (*c*.429-347 BC)

The Greek philosopher, much influenced by Socrates.

After the latter's death in 399, he travelled widely before returning to Athens in *c*.387 and founding the Academy. Here he spent the last forty years of his life, devoting himself to teaching and writing.

His *Dialogues* are the first un-fragmentary body of Greek philosophical writing to have survived, and they had a powerful influence on later philosophers, notably Plotinus. His *Apology* provided a re-creation of the unsuccessful defence which Socrates offered at his trial in 399 BC.

The early *Dialogues*, for example Gorgias and *Protagoras*, examine the question of the essence of virtue and represent a serious questioning of current philosophical thought.

These works adopted Socrates' renowned method of argument, whereby a protagonist's definition was demonstrated to be untrue by a logical series of questions and answers. In the later Dialogues, however, the figure of Socrates served more as a mouthpiece for Plato's developing ideas.

Thus in the *Republic* he tackled the question of the perfect constitution, arguing that perfect unity would come not through democracy, but through the rule of the enlightened despot. In the *Laws* he rejected the excesses of Athenian democracy and argued that extremes of government were to be avoided.

In metaphysics, Plato's Theory of Forms (see universals), introduced in the *Phaedo*, postulated the existence of unchanging and eternal objects; each Form Plato regarded as the indivisible essence of a particular thing or concept. For example, particular objects *are* tables, are called 'tables' and can be recognized as such because they are related to the essential Form of the Table.

Plato's teachings had a profound influence both on Aristotle and on several Roman authors, notably Cicero, shaping the development of Christian theology and Western philosophy. His works were translated into Latin in the late 15th century and became central to Renaissance scholarship and ideas.

Pericles (*c.*495-429 BC)

The Athenian statesman and general, noted for his oratory, political acumen, and integrity, he dominated Athens throughout the third quarter of the 5th century BC. He supported Ephialtes in his attack on the Areopagus, and after his death became champion of the Athenian democracy, proposing pay for jurors, and other innovations.

He was instrumental in strengthening and extending the Athenian empire, sending out colonies, and personally leading the attack against rebellions at Samos and an expedition into the Black Sea, important as a source of corn.

He originated a major building programme, of which the jewel was the Parthenon, the temple which dominated the acropolis. When the spectre of war with the Peloponnesians threatened in the 430s, Pericles determined to resist their demands.

After the Peloponnesian War broke out, he persuaded the Athenians to abandon the countryside when the Spartans invaded and to rely on their fleet. He was briefly deposed from the generalship when plague shattered Athenian confidence, but was re-elected the following year (429). He died of plague soon afterwards.

Aristotle (384-322 BC)

One of the most celebrated Greek philosophers.

At the age of 17 he joined Plato's Academy, where he stayed until shortly after Plato's death in 347. He was later (343-2) appointed tutor to Alexander the Great.

In 335 he returned to Athens, where he established a school and a collection of manuscripts which was the model for later libraries. He organised research projects, the fruit of one being a comparative study of 158 Greek constitutions.

Following the death of Alexander in 323, he was charged with impiety and left Athens, dying soon afterwards in Chalcis.

His output was enormous and survives largely in the form of notes for lectures delivered at the Lyceum, successor to Plato's Academy.

Aristotle's work encompasses:

1. Dialogues which exist only in fragments;

2. collections of historical information;

3. the extant *Constitution of the Athenians* (though the authorship of this is now doubted); and

4. scientific and philosophical works which are mostly extant, such as the *Nicomachaean Ethics*, the *Politics*, and the *Metaphysics*, some of which reveal the influence of Plato.

These writings reveal the encyclopaedic nature of Aristotle's interests and his logical, carefully organized work laid the foundations of many later philosophical enquiries.

He introduced the systematic study of logic, developing a system for describing and assessing reasoning that remained the core of the discipline until the 19th century. Contemporary categorial grammar can be traced to Aristotle's interest in the functioning of words, giving him a special place in philosophical logic and in linguistics.

The central questions of Aristotle's *Metaphysics* (What is substance?) and his *On Coming to be and Passing Away* (How do things come into existence and cease to exist?) are still hotly debated. In *De Anima* (On the

Soul) Aristotle discussed the soul, or psyche; that which makes something alive and capable of the activities characteristic of life.

In claiming that the psyche is dependent upon the body, Aristotle anticipated the mind/body debate current in philosophy of mind. Contemporary ethics also owes a debt to Aristotle's *Ethics*.

His claim that all action aims at *eudaimonia*, or happiness, seemingly has much in common with modern-day utilitarianism; however, Aristotle's stress on the several virtues is in tension with utilitarianism's promise of a single (if not simple) principle for deciding all moral questions.

Aristotle's work was rediscovered by Arab scholars, notably Avicenna and Averroes, and, translated into Latin, shaped the development of medieval thought in the arts and sciences. St Thomas Aquinas reconciled the Aristotelian doctrines with those of Christian theology and they remained a key part of higher education in Europe from the 13th to the 17th centuries.

Intellectual roots

Conservatism

Conservatism is a political doctrine that emphasizes the value of traditional institutions and practices.

Conservatism is a preference for the historically inherited rather than the abstract and ideal. This preference has traditionally rested on an organic conception of society—that is, on the belief that society is not merely a loose collection of individuals but a living organism comprising closely connected, interdependent members.

Conservatives thus favour institutions and practices that have evolved gradually and are manifestations of continuity and stability. Government's responsibility is to be the servant, not the master, of existing ways of life, and politicians must therefore resist the temptation to transform society and politics.

This suspicion of government activism distinguishes conservatism not only from radical forms of political thought but also from liberalism, which is a modernizing, anti-traditionalist movement dedicated to correcting the evils and abuses resulting from the misuse of social and political power.

In *The Devil's Dictionary* (1906), the American writer Ambrose Bierce cynically (but not inappropriately) defined the conservative as "a statesman who is enamoured of existing evils, as distinguished from the Liberal, who wishes to replace them with others."

Conservatism must also be distinguished from the reactionary outlook, which favours the restoration of a previous, and usually outmoded, political or social order.

General characteristics

A common way of distinguishing conservatism from both liberalism and radicalism is to say that conservatives reject the optimistic view that human beings can be morally improved through political and social change.

Conservatives who are Christians sometimes express this point by saying that human beings are guilty of original sin. Sceptical conservatives merely observe that human history, under almost all imaginable political and social circumstances, has been filled with a great deal of evil.

Far from believing that human nature is essentially good or that human beings are fundamentally rational, conservatives tend to assume that human beings are driven by their passions and desires—and are therefore naturally prone to selfishness, anarchy, irrationality, and violence.

Accordingly, conservatives look to traditional political and cultural institutions to curb humans' base and destructive instincts. In Burke's words, people need "a sufficient restraint upon their passions," which it is the office of government "to bridle and subdue."

Families, churches, and schools must teach the value of self-discipline, and those who fail to learn this lesson must have discipline imposed upon them by government and law. Without the restraining power of such institutions, conservatives believe, there can be no ethical behaviour and no responsible use of liberty.

Conservatism is as much a matter of temperament as of doctrine. It may sometimes even accompany left-wing politics or economics—as it did, for example, in the late 1980s, when hard-line communists in the Soviet Union were often referred to as "conservatives."

Typically, however, the conservative temperament displays two characteristics that are scarcely compatible with communism.

The first is a distrust of human nature, rootlessness (social disconnectedness), and untested innovations, together with a corresponding trust in unbroken historical continuity and in the traditional frameworks for conducting human affairs. Such frameworks may be political, cultural, or religious, or they may have no abstract or institutional expression at all.

The second characteristic of the conservative temperament, which is closely related to the first, is an aversion to abstract argument and theorizing. Attempts by philosophers and revolutionaries to plan society in advance, using political principles purportedly derived from reason alone, are misguided and likely to end in disaster, conservatives say. In this respect the conservative temperament contrasts markedly with that of the liberal. Whereas the liberal consciously articulates abstract theories, the conservative instinctively embraces concrete traditions.

For just this reason, many authorities on conservatism have been led to deny that it is a genuine ideology, regarding it instead as a relatively inarticulate state of mind. Whatever the merits of this view, it remains true that the best insights of conservatism seldom have been developed into sustained theoretical works comparable to those of liberalism and radicalism.

In opposition to the "rationalist blueprints" of liberals and radicals, conservatives often insist that societies are so complex that there is no reliable and predictable connection between what governments try to do and what actually happens.

It is therefore futile and dangerous, they believe, for governments to interfere with social or economic realities—as happens, for example, in government attempts to control wages, prices, or rents.

The claim that society is too complex to be improved through social engineering naturally raises the question, "What kind of understanding of society is possible?" The most common conservative answer emphasises the idea of tradition.

People are what they are because they have inherited the skills, manners, morality, and other cultural resources of their ancestors.

An understanding of tradition—specifically, a knowledge of the history of one's own society or country—is therefore the most valuable cognitive resource available to a political leader, not because it is a source of abstract lessons but because it puts him directly in touch with the society whose rules he may be modifying.

Conservative influences operate indirectly—i.e., other than via the programs of political parties—largely by virtue of the fact that there is much in the general human temperament that is naturally or instinctively conservative, such as the fear of sudden change and the tendency to act habitually.

These traits may find collective expression in, for example, a resistance to imposed political change and in the entire range of convictions and preferences that contribute to the stability of a particular culture.

In all societies, the existence of such cultural restraints on political innovation constitutes a fundamental conservative bias, the implications of which were aphoristically expressed by the 17th-century English statesman Viscount Falkland: "If it is not necessary to change, it is necessary not to change."

Mere inertia, however, has rarely sufficed to protect conservative values in an age dominated by rationalist dogma and by social change related to continuous technological progress.

Conservatism has often been associated with traditional and established forms of religion. After 1789 the appeal of religion redoubled, in part because of a craving for security in an age of chaos.

The Roman Catholic Church, because of its roots in the Middle Ages, has appealed to more conservatives than has any other religion. Although he was not a Catholic, Burke praised Catholicism as "the most effectual barrier" against radicalism. But conservatism has had no dearth of Protestant, Jewish, Islamic, and strongly anticlerical adherents.

Intellectual roots of conservatism

Although conservatives sometimes claim philosophers as ancient as Aristotle and Cicero as their forebears, the first explicitly conservative political theorist is generally considered to be Edmund Burke.

In 1790, when the French Revolution still seemed to promise a bloodless utopia, Burke predicted in his *Reflections on the Revolution in France*—and not by any lucky blind guess but by an analysis of its rejection of tradition and inherited values—that the revolution would descend into terror and dictatorship.

In their rationalist contempt for the past, he charged, the revolutionaries were destroying time-tested institutions without any assurance that they could replace them with anything better.

Political power is not a license to rebuild society according to some abstract, untested scheme; it is a trust to be held by those who are mindful of both the value of what they have inherited and of their duties to their inheritors. For Burke, the idea of inheritance extended far beyond property to include language, manners and morals, and appropriate responses to the human condition.

To be human is to inherit a culture, and politics cannot be understood outside that culture. In contrast to the Enlightenment philosophers Thomas Hobbes, John Locke, and Jean-Jacques Rousseau, each of whom conceived of political society as based on a hypothetical social contract among the living.

Because the social contract as Burke understood it involves future generations as well as those of the present and the past, he was able to urge improvement through political change, but only as long as the change is evolutionary: "A disposition to preserve and an ability to improve, taken together, would be my standard of a statesman."

Burke's conservatism was not an abstract doctrine; it represented the particular conservatism of the unwritten British constitution. In the politics of his time Burke was a Whig, and he bequeathed to later conservative thinkers the Whig belief in limited government.

Burke shocked his contemporaries by insisting with brutal frankness that "illusions" and "prejudices" are socially necessary. He believed that most human beings are innately depraved, steeped in original sin, and unable to better themselves with their feeble reason.

Better, he said, to rely on the "latent wisdom" of prejudice, which accumulates slowly through the years, than to "put men to live and trade each on his own private stock of reason."

Among such prejudices are those that favour an established church and a landed aristocracy; members of the latter, according to Burke, are the "great oaks" and "proper chieftains" of society, provided that they temper their rule with a spirit of timely reform and remain within the constitutional framework.

In Burke's writings the entire political wisdom of Europe is formulated in a new idiom, designed to bring out the folly of French revolutionaries intoxicated by sudden power and abstract ideas of a perfect society.

For Burke, modern states are so complex that any attempt to reform them on the basis of metaphysical doctrines alone is bound to end in despotism.

The passion and eloquence with which he developed this argument contributed significantly to the powerful conservative reactions against the French Revolution throughout Europe in the late 18th and early 19th centuries.

Conservatism in the 19th century

The 19th century was in many ways antithetical to conservatism, both as a political philosophy and as a program of particular parties identified with conservative interests.

The Enlightenment had engendered widespread belief in the possibility of improving the human condition—a belief, that is, in the idea of progress—and a rationalist disposition to tamper with or discard existing institutions or practices in pursuit of that goal.

The French Revolution gave powerful expression to this belief, and the early Industrial Revolution and advances in science reinforced it. The resulting rationalist politics embraced a broad segment of the political spectrum, including liberal reformism, trade-union socialism (or social democracy), and ultimately Marxism.

In the face of this constant rationalist innovation, conservatives often found themselves forced to adopt a merely defensive role, so that the political initiative lay always in the other camp.

Conservatism and nationalism

Industrialisation hastened the decline of old-style conservatism because it tended to strengthen the commerce-minded middle class and to create a new industrial working class with a diminished allegiance to old institutions.

Between 1830 and 1880 liberalism won repeated victories over the conservative establishment in Western Europe. Conservatives, like other political groups, had to establish majorities in parliament if they wanted to hold power, and the progressive expansion of the franchise meant that they had to cultivate support from a broad electorate.

But their chief source of strength, the rural peasantry, was declining in numbers relative to other social groups and was in any case too small to support an effective national party.

Conservative parties eventually solved this problem by identifying themselves with nationalist sentiments. This strategy was pursued most vigorously in Germany, where the unification of the German states into a single nation became a central preoccupation of both liberals and conservatives by the middle of the 19th century.

The Prussian chancellor Otto von Bismarck used nationalist sentiments stirred up by Prussia's successful wars against Denmark (1864), Austria (1866), and France (1870–71) to create a united Germany under the Prussian monarchy in 1871.

The conservative governments he headed as Germany's chancellor for the next 20 years undertook various social welfare measures—such as pensions and unemployment benefits—to draw working-class support away from the leftist Social Democratic Party.

Although Bismarck protected the dominant position of the Prussian landowning (Junker) and officer classes, his social welfare measures mitigated class conflict and facilitated a social cohesion in Germany that lasted to the end of World War I.

By the end of the 19th century, conservative parties throughout Europe had adopted the nationalist strategy. This gave them increased popular appeal in an era of intensifying patriotic feeling, but it also contributed to the climate of international rivalry that culminated in the outbreak of World War I in 1914. Conservative parties were almost invariably the staunchest and most intractable supporters of this war.

Conservatism since the turn of the 20th century

The Allied victory in World War I resulted in the downfall of four great imperial dynasties—those in Russia, Austria-Hungary, Germany, and Ottoman Turkey—that were the last major bastions of conservatism based on monarchy, landed aristocracy, and an established church.

After the war, conservative parties became the standard-bearers of frustrated nationalism in Germany as well as in Italy and other former Allied countries. In a process that began in the 1930s and intensified during World War II, conservative parties across central and Eastern Europe were destroyed or co-opted by the totalitarian regime of Nazi Germany.

European conservative parties began to recover their strength only after 1946, and then only in western

Europe, since Soviet power had extirpated all conservative political organizations in eastern Europe.

To the chagrin of western European socialists, conservative parties—or, more commonly, Christian Democratic parties in which various moderate and conservative elements had coalesced—began to win elections in West Germany and other countries.

After the defeat of the fascist regimes, and given socialism's apparent inability to speedily rebuild shattered post-war economies, many Europeans turned once more to conservative policies, which seemed to promise both economic growth and democratic freedoms. This revived conservatism was by now completely shorn of its old aristocratic associations.

Instead, it emphasized the raising of living standards through a market economy and the provision of a wide array of social services by the state. For the rest of the century conservative parties were characterized by liberal individualism tinged with a strong sense of social conscience—as well as by an implacable opposition to communism.

Assessment and prospects

Division, not unity, marked conservatism around the world during the first decade of the 21st century—this despite the defeat of conservatism's chief nemesis of the previous 50 years, Soviet communism.

But perhaps this fissure is not surprising. Anticommunism was the glue that held the conservative movement together, and without this common enemy the many differences between conservatives became all too painfully clear.

In Europe, for example, conservatives split over issues such as the desirability of a united Europe, the advantages of a single European currency (the euro, introduced in the countries of the European Union in 2002), and the region's proper role in policing troubled areas such as the Balkans and the Middle East.

Conservatism was even more divided in the United States. Abortion, immigration, national sovereignty, "family values," and the "war on terror," both at home and abroad, were among the issues that rallied supporters but divided adherents into various camps, from neoconservatives and "paleo-conservatives" (descendants of the Old Right, who regarded neo-conservatives as socially liberal and imperialistic in foreign affairs) to cultural traditionalists among "religious right" groups such as the Christian Coalition and Focus on the Family.

The camps battled one another as well as their perceived enemies in the so-called "culture wars" from the 1990s through the first decade of the 21st century. By the time of the Congressional elections of 2006 and the presidential election of 2008, however, it was clear that such infighting had taken its toll.

Two military invasions and occupations abroad, in Afghanistan and Iraq, had proved enormously expensive in American lives and treasure and cast doubt on the wisdom of the neoconservatives' call for a more interventionist U.S. foreign policy backed by military might.

While American conservatives had long called for smaller government, balanced budgets, and leaving education to the states, the policies of the putatively conservative George W. Bush administration contradicted those key tenets of conservatism.

The global economic crisis that began in 2007–08, during the final year of the Bush administration, turned Americans' attention away from cultural issues such as same-sex marriage and toward more material concerns.

The "new New Deal" introduced by Democratic Pres. Barack Obama's administration in 2009 angered and upset many conservatives, whose ranks nevertheless remained divided.

Government Systems

Monarchy, Aristocracy, Democracy, Oligarchy

- Typology: classification system for claiming broad similarities or differences

- Aristotle's typology based on two questions:

    - Who rules?

    - In whose interest?

Who Rules	Lawful (common good)	Lawless (private interest)
One	Monarchy	Tyranny
Few	Aristocracy	Oligarchy
Many	Polity	Democracy

- modern concept of "democracy" = polity — constitutional democracy

- Dickerson and Flanagan's modern typology

    - Political System:

- **Liberal Democracy**

- **Transitional Democracies**

- **Autocratic** (authoritarian &
  totalitarian)

- **Institutions** — relationship between
legislative (make laws) & executive (enforce laws &
enforce laws)

- **Parliamentary / Presidential /
  Hybrid**

- **Unitary / Devolution / Federalism /
  Confederation**

-

Liberal democracies

- form of political system which emerged in
Northern & Western Europe, and European North
America

- "a system of government in which people rule
themselves, either directly or indirectly (through
chosen officials) but in either case subject to
constitutional restraints on the power of the
majority" (D&F, 269)

- **Robert Dahl argues historic sources include:**

- **Greek city-state: assemblies, officials
  elected by lottery**

- Roman Empire & Italian city-states: election of important officials

- Northern Europe: *Ting* (local assemblies) and *Althing* (national assembly); elected king responsible to Ting and limits on his power; equality among citizens

- commonality: limited to 'free men'; oppressive of 'others', esp. women; often popular rule gave way to one-person or one-group rule; only few participated or believed in the underlying 'logic'

- four operating principles:

  - 1. equality of political rights: right to vote and right to engage in civic duties & public offices

  - 2. majority rule: each vote counts equally, so majority vote wins

    - majority = 50%+1

    - plurality = the most

    - qualified majority = certain number above 50%+1

    - unanimity = everyone agrees / votes for the same option

  - 3. political partication: representative democracy

- population votes for leaders who rule

- leaders rule (laws & policy & expenditures) within the constraints of the law

- vs. direct democracy: everyone takes part and votes on all laws & policy & expenditures

- some other options: referendum, initiative & recall (D&F 274-275)

- 4. Political freedom: rights to engage in political activities (speech, writing, organizing, election, etc.)

Autocracies

- Means 'self-rule', but refers to absolute rule by one person or group without limits imposed by law, political institutions, etc.

- various types of autocracy:

    - despotism: one person rule through fear

    - authoritarianism: "authority that may or may not rest on wide popular support but that is not put to the test of free eletions" (D&F 309)

- most are statist:

  - state is final controller of politics, economics, and society is engage in engineering all three directly or indirectly (right-wing and left-wing)

  - do what they think works for the state (regardless of ideology)

Right Wing	Left Wing	
no to limited political pluralism	no to limited political pluralism	
no ideology, but anti-communist	official ideology, anti-captalist & anti-liberal	
limited political mobilization	massive political mobilisation	
no pre-existing plan for social transformation	pre-existing plan for social transformation	
favourable to capitalism	favourable to socialism	

- Totalitarianism is different from both because:
  - focussed on personality of one person — 'cult of personality'
  - reduces the problem or solution to one factor
  - one party state, loyalty to party from all social institutions & people
  - monopolize ideas
  - widespread use of terror
  - state overrides laws & not bound by them
  - planned & controlled economy
- Problems of all systems:
  - elite rule: unnecessary evil or necessary evil?
  - majority v minority rights
  - public interest (common good) v private interest (individual or group interest): what counts as what? eg. private property, national defence, public education
  - how much political autonomy? — state, individuals, groups, etc.
  - how much state intervention in the economy and society?
  - how much political participation of 'non-state' actors, eg. business, unions, etc.?

Highest class

Aristocracy

Aristocracy is the highest class in certain societies, typically comprising people of noble birth holding hereditary titles and offices.

The concept evolved in Ancient Greece, whereby a council of leading citizens was commonly empowered and contrasted with representative democracy, in which a council of citizens was appointed as the "senate" of a city state or other political unit.

The Greeks did not like the concept of monarchy, and as their democratic system fell, aristocracy was upheld.[1] In the 1651 book *Leviathan*, Thomas Hobbes describes an aristocracy as a commonwealth in which the representative of the citizens is an assembly by part only.

It is a system in which only a small part of the population represents the government; "certain men distinguished from the rest". Modern depictions of aristocracy tend to regard it not as the ancient Greek concept of rule by the best, but more as an oligarchy or plutocracy—rule by the few or the wealthy.

The concept of aristocracy per Plato, has an ideal state ruled by the philosopher king. Plato describes these "philosopher kings" as "those who love the sight of truth" (Republic 475c) and supports the idea with the analogy of a captain and his ship or a doctor and his medicine. According to him, sailing and health are not things that everyone is qualified to practice by nature. A large part of the Republic then addresses how the educational system should be set up to produce these philosopher kings.

History of aristocracy

Aristocracies dominated political and economic power for most of the medieval and modern periods almost everywhere in Europe, using their wealth, control of the best land, and control of their tenants to form a powerful political force.

In the 19th century the rising middle class produced rich businessmen, many of whom use their money to buy into the aristocracy.

However, after the 1830s, in country after country, the aristocracies tended to lose their historic dominance over wealth and political power.

The French Revolution in the 1790s forced many aristocrats into exile, relieving them of their lands and power.

After the defeat of Napoleon in 1814, however, the exiles returned but they never recovered all their lands and never wielded as much political power.

Beginning with Britain, Belgium, and Germany, industrialization in the 19th century brought urbanization, with the wealth increasingly concentrated in the cities, which increasingly took political power.

Before 1789, aristocracies were typically closely associated with the church, especially the Catholic Church, but in the 19th century wave after wave of attacks on the Catholics weekend that element of the aristocratic coalition.

As late as 1900, aristocrats maintained political dominance in Britain, Germany, Austria and Russia, but it was more precarious. World War I had the effect of dramatically reducing the power of the aristocrats in all major countries.

In Russia they were expelled by the Communists. After 1900, Liberal and socialist governments levied heavy taxes on landowners, spelling their loss of economic power.

Plutocracy

Great wealth ruling

A plutocracy or plutarchy is a society that is ruled or controlled by people of great wealth or income. The first known use of the term in English dates from 1631.

Unlike systems such as democracy, capitalism, socialism or anarchism, plutocracy is not rooted in an established political philosophy.

Historic examples of plutocracies include the Roman Empire, some city-states in Ancient Greece, the civilization of Carthage, the Italian city-states/merchant republics of Venice, Florence, pre-French Revolution Kingdom of France, Genoa, and the pre-World War II Empire of Japan (the *zaibatsu*).

According to Noam Chomsky and Jimmy Carter, the modern day United States resembles a plutocracy, though with democratic forms. Former Chairman of the federal reserve, Paul Volcker, also believes the US is developing into a plutocracy.

One modern, formal example of a plutocracy, according to some critics, is the City of London. The City (also called the Square Mile of ancient London, corresponding to the modern financial district, an area of about 2.5 km²) has a unique electoral system for its local administration, separate from London proper.

More than two-thirds of voters are not residents, but rather representatives of businesses and other bodies that occupy premises in the City, with votes distributed according to their numbers of employees.

The principal justification for this arrangement is that most of the services provided by the City of London Corporation are used by the businesses in the City. In fact about 450,000 non-residents constitute the city's day-time population, far outnumbering the City's 7,000 residents.

Rule by the wealthy

Plutocracy means 'rule by the wealthy.' It's when a small group consisting of the wealthiest people in a society rule by virtue of their wealth.

Plutocracy is a self-reinforcing system. That is, once a group of wealthy people are in charge, they can use their wealth and political power to change the rules (laws and systems) to make sure that they only get more wealth and power, never less.

Plutocracy isn't exactly a political philosophy, since no one defends it. The word is used as a *pejorative*, or insult, to describe a system that nearly everyone agrees is unjust.

Plutarchy is a society that is ruled or controlled by people of great wealth or income. The first known use of the term in English dates from 1631. Unlike systems such as democracy, capitalism, socialism or anarchism, plutocracy is not rooted in an established political philosophy.

History of Plutocracy

Plutocracy is the oldest form of government in the world. Long before the modern age of science, capitalism, and democracy, people were ruled by powerful, wealthy leaders who because they had all the resources.

Pre-capitalist and non-capitalist societies had or have various forms of social organisation, some based on wealth, but not all. For example, there have been many tribal societies in which the leader is the person who *gives away* the most, not the person who *owns* the most.

For example, the Anglo-Saxons leaders had to earn their followers through generosity and by leading men successfully in battle. Saxon kings gave the spoils of battle to their followers and kept little for themselves and what they did keep were usually gifts from others in the tribe.

There were many other forms of economy in Europe and the rest of the world before trade naturally evolved into the modern competitive market-based system. The development of capitalism differs from other systems in that everyone has equal rights to own, buy, and sell goods. Therefore, under capitalism, any individual may be able to acquire enough wealth to influence politics in their favour.

Thus, while this system creates the most opportunities to make wealth, it also opens the door to plutocracy. This has happened in many places; Florence is a notable example, as the incredibly wealthy Medici family effectively ruled the city for much of the 15th and 16th centuries. Even in supposedly non-capitalist nations, such as modern China, capitalism has enabled many people to gain power.

Today, plutocracy is hotly-debated—the question of whether one nation or another is becoming plutocratic — a concern not only in capitalist countries like the UK and the USA, but also in post-Communist countries like Russia and China, and neutral countries like India.

People are justly concerned about the fact that a tiny percentage of the population has the vast majority of the wealth, and obviously this gives them political power, and it does get used. The questions are only whether these wealthy elite really can or do use their wealth to rule the world in general, and whether the citizens have the right or the need to oppose them.

Many people believe that some plutocracy is a fair trade in exchange for economic development. Also, many people believe that those who become wealthy through business are inherently superior and therefore well-suited to rule. Needless to say, this is not a popular belief.

Capitalism and Plutocracy

Some critics of capitalism feel that it *inevitably* leads to plutocracy without strong protections in place to prevent this; others feel that plutocracy is only a *possible* outcome of unfettered capitalism, not an inevitable result.

Examples:

Capitalism rewards those who gain wealth using what they own: if you own a ship, you can use it to bring your goods to foreign lands and sell them at high prices. Eventually you may earn enough to hire a captain and then all your income will come from your *ownership* of the vessel rather than from you doing any work.

Imagine now that you acquire a whole fleet of ships and that your children inherit them when you die. Now your children have all the income they could ever need, and they never have to work for it, and if they hire wealth managers they can become even *more* wealthy without any personal labour.

Some people find this unjust, while others find it perfectly just, and this is the source of some bitter controversies in the modern era.

But the controversy gets even more complicated, because now that your children have so much free time, they can dedicate themselves to political activism on a level that their poorer fellow-citizens can't match: they can donate massively to campaigns, and spend time shaking hands and gaining influence in the capital, and thus try to skew the system in their favour.

Some people argue that this is justified because you worked hard for your money and your children deserve to have power and influence as a consequence of what you did. Others argue that it's unjust because the children *themselves* didn't earn the money, but only inherited it.

Social useful purposes

Philanthropy is a voluntary, organised effort intended for socially useful purposes.

Philanthropic groups existed in the ancient civilisations of the Middle East, Greece, and Rome: an endowment supported Plato's Academy (*c.* 387 BCE) for some 900 years; the Islamic *waqf* (religious endowment) dates to the 7th century AD; and the medieval Christian church administered trusts for benevolent purposes.

Merchants in 17th- and 18th-century Western Europe founded organisations for worthy causes. Starting in the late 19th century, large personal fortunes led to the creation of private foundations that bequeathed large gifts in support of the arts, education, medical research, public policy, social services, environmental programs, and other causes.

Philanthropy consists of "private initiatives, for the public good, focusing on quality of life".

Philanthropy contrasts with business initiatives, which are private initiatives for private good, focusing on material gain, and with government endeavours, which are public initiatives for public good, e.g., focusing on provision of public services.

Philanthropy is different from *charity,* though there is some overlap. Charity aims to relieve the pain of a particular social problem, whereas philanthropy attempts to address the root cause of the problem.

Philanthropist

A person who practices philanthropy is a philanthropist. This is a person who desires to promote the welfare of others, expressed especially by the generous donation of money to good causes.

World-wide Notable philanthropists

(In alphabetical sequence)

- Abdul Rahman Al-Sumait - founder of Direct Aid, a charity organization that has built 124 hospitals and dispensaries, 840 schools, 204 Islamic centers, 214 women training centers and 2,200 mosques in Africa, has distributed thousands of tons of food and medicines in famine-stricken areas, and has adopted nearly 10,000 orphans.

- Abdul Sattar Edhi - co-head of the Edhi Foundation in Pakistan

- Achyuta Samanta - founder of the Kalinga Institute of Social Sciences (KISS)

- Ailsa Mellon-Bruce - co-founder of the Andrew W. Mellon Foundation

- **Alagappa Chettiar** - notable for work on Indian education

- **Anne-Françoise de Fougeret (1745-1813)**, was a French philanthropist.

- **Alfred Nobel** - founder of the Nobel Prizes

- **Alicia Keys** - American singer/songwriter; spokeswoman for Keep A Child Alive

- **Amal Hijazi** - Lebanese singer, known for her philanthropy

- **Andrew Carnegie** - donated money to build over 2500 libraries worldwide; founder of the Carnegie Foundations, Carnegie Endowment for International Peace, and Carnegie Mellon University

- **Angelina Jolie** - American actress; known for her humanitarian work worldwide; a Goodwill Ambassador for the UN Refugee Agency

- **Anthony Ashley Cooper, 7th Earl of Shaftesbury** - chairman of the Ragged Schools Union (during the Victorian era)

- **Anthony J. Drexel** - founder of Drexel University

- **Arinze Madueke** – doctor, businessman and philanthropist

- **Arpad Busson** - founder of Ark (Absolute Return for Kids) Academy

- Belinda Stronach - co-founder of Spread the Net

- Ben Delo took the The Giving Pledge. His philanthropy follows the philosophy of effective altruism. He wants to use his donations "to safeguard future generations and protect the long-term prospects of humanity".[5]

- Bill Ackman - in 2011, the Ackmans were among *The Chronicle of Philanthropy*'s "Philanthropy 50" list of the most generous donors[6]

- Bill Gates - co-founder of the Bill & Melinda Gates Foundation

- Bilquis Edhi - co-head of the Edhi Foundation in Pakistan

- Bono - one of the world's best-known philanthropic performers; named the most politically effective celebrity of all time by the *National Journal*[7]

- Calvin Lo - has set up different charitable trusts worth US$245 million for his philanthropic initiatives, an amount that rivals many of the long established endowments in Asia.

- Cari Tuna, co-founded Good Ventures

- Catherine T. MacArthur - co-founder of the MacArthur Foundation

- Charles Pratt - founder of Pratt Institute

- Charles Simonyi - founder of Charles and Lisa Simonyi Fund for Arts and Sciences, $100 million

- Chris Martin - lead singer of British alternative rock band Coldplay; known for supporting the Make Trade Fair campaign; he and his band contribute 15% of their money to charity

- Christopher Reeve - founder of the Christopher and Dana Reeve Foundation

- Chuck Feeney - founder of Atlantic Philanthropies

- Cornelius Vanderbilt - funded Vanderbilt University

- Dame Shirley Porter - Tesco heiress; co-founder of *The Porter Foundation*; has donated to Tel Aviv University, social welfare facilities and ecological funding, the National Portrait Gallery in London

- David Bohnett - founder of the David Bohnett Foundation supporting a wide range of social issues including LGBT rights

- David Gilmour - singer and guitarist of Pink Floyd; was made CBE for his years of philanthropy; gave $7.5 million from sale of his London home to the homeless charity Crisis

- David Koch - founder of the David H. Koch Charitable Foundation; listed by *The Chronicle of Philanthropy* as one of the world's top 50 philanthropists in 2013

- Demi Lovato - provides the Lovato Treatment Scholarship; supporter of 13 different charity organization; an official Ambassador for the youth empowerment event We Day and the organization Free the Children

- Dolly Parton - country singer; advocate for children's education through her foundation, the Imagination Library, which gives books to children to develop their reading skills before starting school.

- Don Ball - Co-founder of Ballhomes, founder of Hope Center

- Donald Rix - BC Innovation Council, BC Cancer Agency Foundation, BC Medical Services Foundation, and the BC Children's Hospital Foundation

- Dr. Mo Ibrahim - founder of telecom company Celtel International; set up the Mo Ibrahim Foundation to encourage better governance in Africa, and providing higher education scholarships for leadership and management for Africans; initiated the Mo Ibrahim Prize for Achievement in African Leadership

- Dustin Moskovitz, co-founded Good Ventures

- **Edward Harkness** - various private colleges and boarding schools; medical facilities; Commonwealth Fund

- **Elinor Sauerwein** - Salvation Army philanthropist

- **Ellen Gates Starr** - founder of the biomedical institute that bears his name Hull House

- **Elon Musk** - chairman of the Musk Foundation

- **Elton John** - has raised more than US$125 million just for the Elton John AIDS Foundation. In 2004 he donated over US$43 million to organizations around the world, making him the most generous person in music for that year, "a title he retains year after year." In 1997 he raised US$40 million for charity through sales of the single "Candle in the Wind 1997". He currently supports at least 57 charities.

- **Enriqueta Augustina Rylands** - founder of the John Rylands Library

- **Fazle Hasan Abed** - founder of BRAC

- **Frank F Islam**, information technology entrepreneur, working to improve education system. $2 million invested in Aligarh Muslim University for a separate business school.

- **Gary Sinise** - co-founder of Operation Iraqi Children

- George Clooney - known for humanitarian work in aiding the Darfur conflict, organizing Hope for Haiti Now, and involvement in Not On Our Watch

- George Peabody - considered the father of modern philanthropy, who help to found cultural institutions in the United States and England.

- George Soros - estimated to have donated more than US$6 billion, often through the Open Society Institute and Soros Foundations

- Godwin Maduka, doctor and founder of Las Vegas Pain Institute and Medical Center

- H. F. Lenfest - donated $5 million in coherence with Chester County to preserve over 1,000 acres (4.0 km^2) of land in Newlin Township, Chester County, Pennsylvania; the land is now owned by Natural Lands Trust

- Henry Ford - co-founder of the Ford Foundation

- Henry W. Bloch, Founder of H&R Block Tax company. Henry established the nationally acclaimed Marion Bloch Neuroscience Institute, formed the Marion and Henry Bloch Family Foundation one of the largest family foundations in the region (Midwest) and many other places in the Kansas City community.

- Hilmar Reksten - Norwegian shipping magnate, tax evader, patron of the arts

- Holden Karnofsky, co-founder and board member of the charity evaluator GiveWell and the executive director of the Open Philanthropy Project.

- Howard Ahmanson, Jr. - multi-millionaire philanthropist and financier of the causes of many conservative Christian cultural, religious and political organizations

- Howard Hughes - aviator, engineer, industrialist and film producer; donated US$1.56 billion to various charities including the Howard Hughes Medical Institute

- Iain Percy - co-founder of the Andrew Simpson Sailing Foundation which was set up after the death of his best friend Andrew Simpson to facilitate children's access to sailing

- Imran Khan - founder of the Shaukat Khanum Memorial Trust, which was behind the first cancer research institution in Pakistan

- Irwin M. Jacobs - has contributed hundreds of millions of dollars to the field of education through donations and grants to schools and organizations

- Isaac Wolfson - managing director of Great Universal Stores

- **J. Paul Getty** - funded the construction of the Getty Villa, the original Getty Museum, and donated his art collection to it; upon his death, left his fortune to the Getty Museum, which eventually expanded to the Getty Center in Los Angeles

- **J.K. Rowling** - President of One Parent Families; advocate for social equity

- **James E. Stowers** - founder of the Stowers Institute for Medical Research

- **James Packer** - jointly with his majority-owned company Crown Resorts pledged $200 million over 10 years to support Australian community groups

- **Jamie and Karen Phelps Moyer** - founded the Moyer Foundation to assist non-profit organizations in raising money for children with serious distress

- **Jane Addams** - co-founder of the Hull House settlement house in Chicago

- **Joe Blackman** - Dedicated much of his youth to helping young people start their own businesses

- **John D. MacArthur** - co-founder of the MacArthur Foundation

- **John D. Rockefeller** - founder of the Rockefeller Foundation and Rockefeller University

- **John D. Rockefeller III** - major third-generation Rockefeller philanthropist; founder of the Asia Society (1956), the Population Council (1952) and a reconstituted Japan Society; chairman of the Rockefeller Foundation for 20 years; established the Rockefeller Public Service Awards in 1958

- **John D. Rockefeller Jr.** - dramatically expanded the Rockefeller Foundation and Rockefeller University; bought and then donated the land in Manhattan upon which the United Nations headquarters was built

- **John Harvard** - one of the founders of Harvard College

- **John R. Hunting**, major contributor to liberal or progressive 527 organizations.

- **John Studzinski** - champion of the homeless and the arts in the UK; founder and owner of the Genesis Foundation

- **Johns Hopkins** - founder of the Johns Hopkins University and the Johns Hopkins Hospital

- **Jon Bon Jovi** - American rock star; founder of The Jon Bon Jovi Soul Foundation in 2006

- **Joseph Rowntree** - founder of the four Rowntree trusts

- **Juliette Gordon Low** - founded Girl Scouts of the USA in 1912 in Savannah, Georgia

- Julius Curtis Lewis, Jr. - made an estimated lifetime donations of US$130 million to various civic, spiritual; charitable organizations, many in Savannah, Georgia

- Kenneth C. Griffin - founder and CEO of Citadel LLC; co-founder of the Kenneth and Anne Griffin Foundation[18]

- Lady Gaga - founder of the Born This Way Foundation, a charity started in 2011

- Larry Ellison - pledged to give more than half the value of his stock in Oracle Corporation to the Bill and Melinda Gates Foundation

- Levi Strauss - gave to many notable foundations of his time; gave to many Jewish synagogues and organizations

- Li Ka-shing - founder and chairman of the Li Ka Shing Foundation, which focuses on capacity empowerment through education and building of a caring society through medical and healthcare related projects; in 2006, pledged to donate one-third of his fortune estimated at over US$10 billion to philanthropic projects

- Linus Pauling - donated time and effort and spent personal funds to bring about the worldwide ban on above-ground nuclear weapons testing

- Marc Benioff - created the 1-1-1 model of integrated corporate philanthropy, by which companies contribute 1 percent of equity, 1 percent of employee hours, and 1 percent of product back to the community

- Marcis Liors Skadmanis, founder of the international calendar day for Non-governmental organizations - World NGO Day, annually observed on 27 February.

- Marian Tompson - co-founder of La Leche League International, a breastfeeding support organization

- Mark Zuckerberg - co-founder of social media network Facebook

- Mary Lee Ware - principal sponsor of the Harvard Museum of Natural History's famous Glass Flowers exhibit; key player in the creation of the New Hampshire Rhododendron State Park

- Mary Louise Milliken Childs - builder of the Milliken Memorial Community House, the first privately donated community house in America

- Melinda Gates - co-founder of the Bill & Melinda Gates Foundation

- Metallica - All Within My Hands Foundation, dedicated to creating sustainable communities by supporting workforce education, the fight against hunger, and other critical local services. They also donate a portion of ticket sales in every city visited to a local charity (predominantly food banks)

- Michael Bloomberg - donations include over US$1.1 billion to Johns Hopkins University

- Michael Dell - established the Michael and Susan Dell Foundation, which focuses on grants, urban education, childhood health and family economic stability

- Michael Jackson - donated more than US$50 million to various foundations and won numerous awards for his humanitarianism; founded the Heal the World Foundation

- Michelle Dilhara - Sri Lankan actress

- Milton Hershey - founded the Milton Hershey School for lower income children; invested millions of dollars

- Mohamed Al-Fayed - founder of The New School at West Heath

- Mohammed bin Rashid Al Maktoum - founder of the Mohammed bin Rashid Global Initiatives, a grouping of some 33 charities, awards and philanthropic entities.

- Mr. T - actor; motivational speaker; donated all his gold to charity

- Nicholas Murray Butler - president of the Carnegie Endowment for International Peace, 1925-1945

- **Onyeka Nnadozie Eze** – businessman and philanthropist

- **Oprah Winfrey** - estimated donations above US$300 million, and founder of Oprah's Angel Network

- **P. K. Subban** - Canadian ice hockey player; donated $10 million to the Montreal Children's Hospital

- **Paul Mellon** - major benefactor of arts and education; co-founder of the Andrew W. Mellon Foundation

- **Paul Newman** - founder of Newman's Own and the Hole in the Wall Gang Camp for seriously ill children; major donations to other charities

- **Paul Walker** - founder of the charity Reach Out Worldwide

- **Peter Cooper** - set up a free college in New York City to help poor people ambitious to improve themselves; Thomas Edison was an early alum[24]

- **Petra Němcová** - Czech supermodel; founder of the Happy Hearts Fund

- **Phil Knight** - co-founder of Nike, Inc.; supporter of Oregon Health & Science University, Stanford University and the University of Oregon

- **Prince Al-Waleed bin Talal** - chairman of investment firm Kingdom Holding Company; pledged US$32bn donation to his philanthropy organization Alwaleed Philanthropies[25]

- **Prince Karim Aga Khan IV** - founder[26] and chairman[27] of the Aga Khan Development Network which focuses on health, education, culture, rural development, institution-building and the promotion of economic development

- **Princess Bernice Pauahi** - left properties to the education of Hawaiian boys and girls in what is now Kamehameha Schools

- **Raymond and Ruth Perelman** - parents of Ronald O. Perelman; in 2011 donated $225 million to the University of Pennsylvania Medical School, the largest donation in that university's history

- **Richard Desmond** - President of the Norwood Charity; raised around £14m for charitable causes with the RD Crusaders; helped build the Richard Desmond Children's Eye Centre part of Moorfields Eye Hospital

- **Rizwan Hussain** - barrister, television presenter, international humanitarian worker; former Hindi music singer and producer; known for presenting Islamic and charity shows on Channel S and Islam Channel

- Ronald O. Perelman - largest Revlon stockholder; has donated over $200 million to various causes since 2001, including a $50 million gift to create the Ronald O. Perelman Heart Institute at New York Presbyterian Hospital and Weill Cornell Medical Center; signed the Gates-Buffett Pledge in August 2010, committing up to half his assets to be designated for the benefit of charitable causes (after his family and children have been provided for)

- Ruth Pfau - head of the Marie Adelaide Leprosy Centre in Pakistan; as a result of her efforts, the World Health Organization declared leprosy a controlled disease in Pakistan in 1996

- Samuel Morley MP - founded Morley College, London; endowed other institutions and causes

- Sandro Salsano - chairman of Salsano Group; founder of Salsano Shahani Foundation

- Sean Parker, donated $600 million to launch the Parker Foundation, which focuses on three areas: Life Sciences, Global Public Health and Civic Engagement ; and donated $250 million to create the Parker Institute for Cancer Immunotherapy

- Shahrukh Khan - the only Indian to receive UNESCO Pyramide con Marni award for his charity work in 2011

- Shakira - founder of Pies Descalzos Foundation

- Sidney Myer - founder of the Australian Department store chain Myer

- Sir Charles Henry de Soysa - Ceylonese entrepreneur who pioneered a multitude of medical, educational, religious and infrastructure projects

- Sir Cliff Richard - one of the vice-presidents of Tearfund, a British religious, relief and development agency; supports The Hunger Project, Kidney Research UK, Roy Castle Lung Cancer Foundation, Teenage Cancer Trust, Cliff Richard Tennis Foundation, Alzheimer's Research UK; opened two new purpose-built buildings for Self Unlimited, a national charity for people with learning disabilities

- Sir David Robinson - founder of the Robinson Charitable Trust and Robinson College

- Sir Ganesh Dutt - longest-serving minister in British Empire who gave all his earnings to charitable works, especially education

- Sir Run Run Shaw - founder of the Shaw Prize Foundation

- Steve Wozniak - provided the money, and some technical support, for technology program for the Los Gatos School district; co-founder of Apple Computer (now Apple Inc.)

- **Sunil Bharti Mittal** - set up Bharti Foundation which runs schools for 30,000 underprivileged children in rural India

- **Tad Taube** - chairman of Taube Philanthropies - https://jshofnc.org/inductees/tad-taube/

- **Tarek Ben Halim** - investment banker and founder of Alfanar in 2004, the first Venture philanthropy organization with a special focus on the Arab world

- **Thomas Holloway** - Victorian patent medicine entrepreneur and founder of Royal Holloway, University of London

- **Ty Pennington** - host of ABC's *Extreme Makeover: Home Edition*; advocate of doing good towards others in need and to those who give of themselves for the sake of others

- **Usher Raymond** - American singer/songwriter; founding Chairman of the New Look Foundation; advocate for social justice

- **Vernon Hill** - founder of Commerce Bank and President of Metro Bank; donated $10m to the Penns School of Veterinary Medicine

- **Vijay Eswaran** - founder of RYTHM foundation and Q NET

- **Virginia Weiffenbach Kettering** - Dayton, Ohio's leading philanthropist and patron of the arts

- **Warren Buffett** - pledged US$30.7 billion worth of Berkshire Hathaway stock to the Bill and Melinda Gates Foundation

- **Werner Reinhart** - industrialist, philanthropist, music and literature patron

- **William Allen** - founded and endowed many institutions and causes including 'Schools of Industry' at Lindfield and Newington Academy for Girls.

- **William Henry Vanderbilt** - co-founder of the Metropolitan Opera

- **William Wilberforce** - English politician; headed successful parliamentary campaign against the British slave trade; later supported the campaign for complete abolition

- **Yusuf Islam** (also known as Cat Stevens) - founder of Islamic schools, Muslim Aid and Small Kindness.

Greatest philanthropists by amount of USD

The following table orders the greatest philanthropists by estimated amount given to charity, corresponding to USD.

Name	Amount given	Cause
<u>Bill Gates</u>	$35.8 billion	Healthcare, extreme poverty, education, access to information technology
<u>Warren Buffett</u>	$34 billion	Healthcare, education, AIDS-prevention, sanitation
<u>Li Ka-shing</u>	$10.7 billion	Education, healthcare
<u>Andrew Carnegie</u>	$9.5 billion	Libraries, education, peace
<u>Azim Premji</u>	$8 billion	Education, healthcare
<u>Chuck Feeney</u>	$6.8 billion	Healthcare, youth, ageing, poverty, human rights

Name	Amount given	Cause
<u>George Soros</u>	$6.1 billion	Healthcare, <u>anti-fascist</u> publications, human rights, economic, legal, and social reform
<u>Alwaleed Philanthropies</u>	$4 billion	Alwaleed Philanthropies collaborates with a range of philanthropic, government and educational organizations to combat poverty, empower women and youth, develop communities, provide disaster relief and create cultural understanding through education.
<u>Phil Knight</u>	$2 billion	Education, healthcare, intercollegiate athletics
<u>James E. Stowers</u>	$2 billion	Healthcare
<u>Howard Hughes</u>	$1.56 billion	Healthcare

Possible future assimilation

With the arrival of the present (year 2020) Coronavirus (Covid-19) pandemic spread the true colours of all classes around the world have shown that there is no difference as to whether one belongs to the upper crust of society, or whether one is rich (surrounded with the goods of his desires) at the end of it all one result remains; human life is meaningless without compassion and benevolence.

With such recent events (the world-wide spreading of the coronavirus) the reader will wonder and conclude as to whether these class distinctions should still exist.

This is human nature and as soon as people overcome the ill effects and constraints of this disabling pandemic then all earth beings will forget the sufferings and worries and will start all over with the financial competitions, conflicts and restrictions to the less fortunate people.

The class of Aristocrats and their peers will still be governing and the Plutocrats will continue to manipulate the class distinctions to suit their personal esteem.

This includes royalties, business gurus, religious leaders, Presidents and Prime Ministers. Further on, the '.com' owners who have incomes and profitability bigger than most countries of the world shall become wealthier.

As for the religious leaders such as the Pope, the Patriarchs, Ayatollahs, and Archbishops are using the wealth of their functions to influence themselves upon their followers; behaving as if they are modern Caesars.

Royalties in certain countries are so wealthy and run businesses with profitability that they can also be called Plutocrats. On the other hand, a few of them rectify their attributes to be called Philanthropists.

Of course, there will be those who gain affluence and esteem based on a day's honest work. This category cannot be included in the class of Plutocrats, in as much as they are the professionals with acumen/s used for the benefit of others, and the progression of living styles.

Whatever the criteria expressed in this book/section, one way or another, people will find their own interpretation of Aristocracy, Plutocracy and Philanthropy.

As such, everybody is allowed free will and freedom of choice.

END

Index   *Page*

Bibliography

ALL BOOKS LISTED BELOW ARE PUBLISHED BY ANDREAS SOFRONIOU

1. THERAPEUTIC PSYCHOLOGY, ISBN: 978-1-326-34523-5
2. MEDICAL ETHICS THROUGH THE AGES, ISBN: 978-1-4092- 7468-1
3. MEDICAL ETHICS, FROM HIPPOCRATES TO THE 21ST CENTURY ISBN: 978-1-4457-1203-1
4. MISINTERPRETATION OF SIGMUND FREUD, ISBN: 978-1-4467-1659-5
5. JUNG'S PSYCHOTHERAPY: THE PSYCHOLOGICAL & MYTHOLOGICAL METHODS, ISBN: 978-1-4477-4740-6
6. FREUDIAN ANALYSIS & JUNGIAN SYNTHESIS, ISBN: 978-1-4477-5996-6
7. ADLER'S INDIVIDUAL PSYCHOLOGY AND RELATED METHODS, ISBN: 978-1-291-85951-5
8. ADLERIAN INDIVIDUALISM , JUNGIAN SYNTHESIS, FREUDIAN ANALYSIS, ISBN: 978-1-291-85937-9
9. PSYCHOTHERAPY, CONCEPTS OF TREATMENT, ISBN: 978-1-291-50178-0
10. PSYCHOLOGY, CONCEPTS OF BEHAVIOUR, ISBN: 978-1-291-47573-9
11. PHILOSOPHY FOR HUMAN BEHAVIOUR, ISBN: 978-1-291-12707-2
12. SEX, AN EXPLORATION OF SEXUALITY, EROS AND LOVE, ISBN: 978-1-291-56931-5
13. PSYCHOLOGY FROM CONCEPTION TO SENILITY, ISBN: 978-1-4092-7218-2
14. PSYCHOLOGY OF CHILD CULTURE, ISBN: 978-1-4092-7619-7
15. JOYFUL PARENTING, ISBN: 0 9527956 1 2
16. GUIDE TO A JOYFUL PARENTING, ISBN: 0 952 7956 1 2
17. THERAPEUTIC PHILOSOPHY FOR THE INDIVIDUAL AND THE STATE, ISBN: 978-1-4092-7586-2
18. PHILOSOPHIC COUNSELLING FOR PEOPLE AND THEIR GOVERNMENTS, ISBN: 978-1-4092-7400-1
19. CHILD PSYCHOTHERAPY, ISBN: 978-1-326-44169-2
20. HYPNOTHERAPY IN MEDICINE, PSYCHOLOGY, MAGIC, ISBN: 978-1-326-48163-6
21. ART FOR PSYCHOTHERAPY, ISBN: 978-1-326-78959-6
22. SLEEPING AND DREAMING EXPLAINED BY ARTS & SCIENCE, ISBN: ISBN: 978-1-326-81309-3
23. PHILOSOPHY AND POLITICS, ISBN: 978-1-326-33854-1
24. MORAL PHILOSOPHY, FROM SOCRATES TO THE 21ST AEON, ISBN: 978-1-4457-4618-0
25. MORAL PHILOSOPHY, FROM HIPPOCRATES TO THE 21ST AEON, ISBN: 978-1-84753-463-7
26. MORAL PHILOSOPHY, THE ETHICAL APPROACH THROUGH THE AGES, ISBN: 978-1-4092-7703-3
27. MORAL PHILOSOPHY, ISBN: 978-1-4478-5037-3
28. 2011 POLITICS, ORGANISATIONS, PSYCHOANALYSIS, POETRY, ISBN: 978-1-4467-2741-6
29. WISDOM AN ACCUMULATION OF KNOWLEDGE, ISBN: 978-1-326-99692-5
30. MYTHOLOGY LEGENDS FROM AROUND THE GLOBE, ISBN: 978-1-326-98630-8
31. PLATO'S EPISTEMOLOGY, ISBN: 978-1-4716-6584-4
32. ARISTOTLE'S AETIOLOGY, ISBN: 978-1-4716-7861-5
33. MARXISM, SOCIALISM & COMMUNISM, ISBN: 978-1-4716-8236-0
34. MACHIAVELLI'S POLITICS & RELEVANT PHILOSOPHICAL CONCEPTS, ISBN: 978-1-4716-

www.ingramcontent.com/pod-product-compliance
Lightning Source LLC
Chambersburg PA
CBHW060437290526
45791CB00002B/970

* 9 7 8 0 2 4 4 8 7 9 8 9 1 *